My Time to Rhyme

Jon N. McCready

*A compendium of recollections, reflections
and musings in verse*

Dedicated to the WORD Who became flesh and dwelt among us – full of grace and truth.

-   John 1:1, 14

Contents

Introduction

When I was a sophomore in high school, my English teacher, Paul Sherrock, took the stage at an assembly one afternoon in the school auditorium and recited from memory "The Shooting of Dan McGrew", a rather lengthy poem by Robert Service. I was spellbound, not just by the story it told, but amazed by his being able to memorize such a lengthy piece of literature. I now believe that some of that was accomplished due to the cadence and rhyming of words that held my attention, as it did that day for most students and faculty alike.

Little at the time did I realize the influence that recitation would have on me, as a number of years passed before I had an occasion to write a poem of my own to my mother, and another to my grandmother. The poems were received with sufficient pleasure to encourage me to attempt doing so on other occasions.

I found that I derived enjoyment out of attempting to tell a story; be it nostalgic, contemplative, humorous, silly, or surprising, using rhythms and rhymes as did Robert Service, Robert Frost, Oliver Wendell Holmes, Thomas Hardy, and Henry Wadsworth Longfellow; some of my favorite writers. I have also enjoyed memorizing over a dozen of their poems to share on occasion.

Some of my poems are spot on true. Others are based on true happenings that are tweaked a bit to fit, while others are pure fantasy. Lastly, I get a kick out of creating an ending to some poems that may be unexpected. I hope these might bring a smile to your face and heart.

These 50 odd poems I leave behind
And hope you find some dandy.
If otherwise, I'll dry my eyes,
But keep my notebook handy.

Then take a pen and try again
To tell a different story.
And hope by gum that you'll find one
You think just hunky-dory.

And if per chance at second glance
A poem may strike you funny,
Don't hesitate; It's not too late
To send a sum of money.

NOTE (Just Kidding)

Part 1
THE EARLY YEARS

Me and my siblings, Nancy, Ken and Mary
in the living room of our new home

Me and sisters Nancy and Mary at Avenue B in
Snohomish, Wa

Nice set of wheels!

"Hey, sis, can I borrow your wheels?"

Child's Play

I'd like once more to be a youth;
To play the games that children play.
Pretend to be a private sleuth,
A movie star, a stowaway.

When I was young we'd build a fort
On some kind neighbors' vacant lot,
And spend the day in valiant sport
Defending ancient Camelot.

We'd pull the ferns from tender ground
And strip them clean except for tail.
Then wing them with a whirring sound,
And drag the captured off to jail.

A game of 'tag', or 'hide and seek'
From dawn 'til dusk was daily fare.
But woe the one who had to peek;
For time not welcome anywhere.

Then 'kick the can', or 'steal the flag';
The simple games I loved the best.
The victors won the right to brag;
The losers faced the acid test.

Parades were fun to organize;
Batons to twirl, and bikes to ride.
The fun of wearing some disguise
From which self-consciousness could hide.

Imagination; that's the key
That opens almost any door.
Without a dream where would we be
With so much life yet to explore.

Sometimes we lose the memory
That youth and fun go hand in hand.
But life provides no guarantee.
Enjoy your youth; aye, it is grand.

I've played the games that children play.
Why must adults be reconciled
To make one think we're so passe'?
I'd trade today to be the child.

Birthday with my buddies in my backyard

When I was quite young, I often heard my sister, Nancy, saying, "Oh, Be Quiet!" as I entered the house. This poem is a play on this very common remark that was often a plea for solitude so she could have a quiet time to enjoy reading her novels. Nancy was two years older than me.

O.B. Quiet

"Oh, Be Quiet!" came the cry;
　　It struck me to the quick.
Then little did I realize
　　That phrase would somehow stick.
My sister seldom raised her voice;
　　It simply wasn't her,
But 'neath the saddle she would sit
　　I was a constant burr.

Whenever I bounced through the door
　　The solitude she sought
Would dissipate in the earthquake
　　That 'O.B. Quiet' brought.
She used the phrase so often that
　　I thought it was my name.
It sounded like a greeting when
　　Into the room I came.

Most often she would be engrossed
    In some romantic book
When 'O.B.' crashed the silence and
    Received a chilling look.
"Mother, can't you make him stop?"
    Would come her woeful plea.
While wondering what life was like
    Without a loud 'O.B.'

But I was just a youngster and
    Could hardly then be blamed
For all the zeal a boy can feel
    When youth has not been tamed.
Yet, now that we're both older we've
    Become the best of friends.
The years have done the softening
    Just like the willow bends.

I'm more sophisticated now;
    She's full of energy.
It's funny how the branches grow
    From out the family tree.
So, if your brother's testing you
    With noise; a steady diet.
Have patience with the little lad.
    Don't call him, "Oh Be Quiet"!

Nancy without a noisy "O.B. Quiet"

The Playhouse

My neighbor had a playhouse
   Kitty-corner 'cross the street
Tucked in beneath some evergreens
   Where all the kids would meet.
Its little door and windows
   Were proportioned to our size
Where we could play our children's games
   Away from grown-up eyes.

The playhouse was the schoolhouse
   Where the oldest was the teacher.
Next time a Sunday schoolroom
   With a Pentecostal preacher.
From day to day and week to week
   We'd play at something new.
It seemed each time we'd get inside
   It came out of the blue.

The playhouse was the fortress
   Of the pirate Escabar,
Who ruled the seas, and sank the ships,
   And plundered near and far.
The wicked Queen of Endor
   Had a very clever way
Of catching unsuspecting souls
   Who often went astray.

One day it was the clubhouse
    Of the Junior Buffaloes.
The next it was the palace
    Of the lovely Princess Rose.
So many days; so many ways,
    The playhouse was our friend.
It never ceased to offer us
    A place we could pretend.

The years have flown so quickly,
    Seems like only yesterday
Someone was knocking at my door
    To ask if I could play.
I hope that playhouse still is there,
    And children use it yet,
To play the games that children play
    So they may not forget.

Playhouse, schoolhouse, clubhouse, fortress,
palace, and friend

The Cottonwood Swing

When I was a lad I used to swing
On a swing that was built for two.
With my sister sitting by my side
We would push for the open blue.

It hung from the giant Cottonwoods
Not far from our kitchen door,
And it wouldn't take very long at all
'Til we'd soon begin to soar.

I could feel the wind blowing in my face
And the butterflies moving round
Somewhere inside where my feelings ride
Climbing farther from the ground.

Higher and higher we climbed the sky
To see just how high we could go.
We'd stretch our toes to the waiting branch
Then back to the earth below.

The time we spent on our swing was meant
For our scrapbook of memories.
Skinned knees and all I like to recall
The swing in the Cottonwood trees.

Swing in the Cottonwood trees on the left

Nancy and me on the Cottonwood swing -
A couple of "real swingers"!

*When I was fairly young I would, on occasion, stand behind a
card table that was laid on its side and pretend it was a pulpit,
from which I could sing, and pretend I was the pastor of the
Methodist church we attended while growing up.*

The Boy Preacher

✝ ✝ ✝ ✝

The boy preacher entered his pulpit;
    A card table laid on its side.
Placed his hands on the corners,
    Then stood with his arms opened wide.
He welcomed the small congregation;
    Two sisters, a dog and a cat
Who waited in anticipation
    On the sofa where all of them sat.

He asked them to turn in their hymnbook
    To page number 423.
Then sang with a great deal of gusto,
    The words, though a little off-key.
He opened the family Bible
    And preached that they all must repent.
They nodded their heads in agreement,
    Though none of them knew what it meant.

He banged with his fist on the table
  The way he remembered it done
The last time he heard Rev. Johnson
  Declare that the battle was won.
And then came the time for the offering;
  Eight pennies were put in the plate.
He offered a prayer of thanksgiving,
  And then noticed the time getting late.

They sang one last song for the closing;
  He offered another short prayer.
Acknowledged their wiggles and squirming,
  And thanked them for all being there.
The sisters departed the parlor
  To play a more feminine game,
While the animals looked at the preacher
  As tho' willing for more of the same.

So the boy preacher practiced his sermon
  With pointing and gestures galore.
The kitten still curled on the sofa;
  The dog now stretched out on the floor.
Well, the animals sure got an earful
  Of what young preacher boy had to say,
But it's doubtful that any repentance
  Took place in the parlor that day.

My folks were very tolerant when I was quite young and allowed me to hang a small basketball net on the back of a kitchen table chair, moved to the living room in the evening, and shoot a tennis ball at the hoop. Fortunately, I never damaged or broke anything. My dad was quite the basketball and tennis player in his younger years, which may be why he was so tolerant of my antics. My sister, Nancy, is the one who coined the phrase, "Here come the Whities".

The Whities

"Here comes the Whities!";
   He's in his underwear.
He deftly sends the tennis ball
   Caroming through the air.
It finds the net around the hoop
   That's fastened to the chair.
He's the up and coming
   Player of tomorrow.

"Here comes the Whities!";
   He dodges left and right.
He moves with such agility,
   This kid is out of sight.
All the human eye can see
   Is just a blur of white.
He's the basketball
   Sensation of the future.

He's guarded by the table lamp;
    He slows down to a walk.
He circles 'round the easy chair,
    And glances at the clock.
Then drives straight for the basket
    Like an 18 year old jock.
He's a talent that has
    All the coaches drooling.

"Here comes the Whities!";
    He sees the score is tied.
He summons all the expertise
    On which he has relied.
There's only seconds left to shoot,
    He's got to hit his stride.
It's the championship
    And he's the star performer.

The living room falls silent as
    The ball sails t'ward the thread.
It then erupts with cheering as
    He puts his team ahead.
The game is won, the day is done,
    And now he's off to bed,
'Til tomorrow night's
    Appearance of the "Whities".

The Sleeping Porch

On the sleeping porch in the summertime
    When the air was warm and sweet
My sister and I in our beds would lie
    And savor this special treat.
On a sleepless night I can still recite
    A story, a riddle, or rhyme
That a sister and brother might share with each other
    For fun in more innocent times.

"There are mice", she said, "just above your head
    Through that trapdoor in the ceiling."
And although I knew that it wasn't true
    It still left an uneasy feeling.
So, in bed I'd lie with one open eye
    Searching shadows in every direction.
I'd snuggle and slide 'neath the covers to hide
    In the hope that they offered protection.

Then in time that fear would disappear
    And a brother must surely get even,
So, I'd tell my sis that beneath her bed
    I could hear a monster breathing.
But that's just one of the kinds of fun
    That the two of us fondly remember
As we turned out lights on those summer nights
    From mid-June until early September.

Now, many a night with the wind just right
    And the Cottonwood leaves were blowing
We could hear a train on the distant plain
    And wonder where it might be going.
A robins' nest was a welcome guest
    In the vines on the windowsill.
And the lights would glow from the streets below
    To our home way up on the hill.

When sleep once more poked its head in the door
    And eyelids and shadows descending,
We'd whisper goodnight; hoped the bugs didn't bite,
    And thank God for the day now ending.
Now there'll always be a small part of me
    That would love to spend one more night
In those old bunk beds for two sleepy heads
    On the porch until dawn's early light.

The sleeping porch years later
minus the bunk beds

Fifth Street Hill

If you ever went sledding on Fifth Street Hill
You'll remember the challenge; remember the thrill.
The moment the runners were laid on the track
It was "Look out below!", there was no turning back.

From Avenue B down to Avenue A
Fifth Street would be closed for the children to play.
The bobsleds, and flyers, and occasional skis
Would soon be appearing when Fifth St. would freeze.

The nights cold and crisp with the temperature drop,
And the new fallen snow firmly packed at the top
Heightened anticipation while waiting in line
That the ride to the bottom would stiffen your spine.

The pitch of the hill sent you speeding below,
And with watering eyes from the wind and the snow
Numb hands gripped the steerage to keep 'er on course
As you fought to control gravitational force.

Faster and faster; you felt you could fly.
Those climbing the hill were a blur passing by.
It took full concentration to focus your mind
With a sled out in front and another behind.

At last reaching bottom but still running strong
You just let 'er coast for another block long.
When finally stopped and back on your feet
You began your return up the hill of Fifth Street.

The trudge to the top had its special reward;
There to gather with friends round the fire that roared
From an old metal barrel where people could bend
Just to work out the kinks as they warmed either end.

Though your face may be frozen and feet may be numb;
The hour growing late, but you're still having fun.
Four layers of clothes one would think was enough,
But by time to go home you'd be chilled to the buff.

The streetlight that hung on the corner would glow
Like a Charles Dickens scene with the fresh fallen snow.
Drink a cup of hot chocolate to help ease the chill
As you watch and you plan your last run down the hill.

It's now just a memory; the city won't close
The street any longer whenever it snows.
Concern for your safety has ended the thrill
Of gathering and sledding upon Fifth Street hill.

Poem published in *Ideals Christmas* magazine

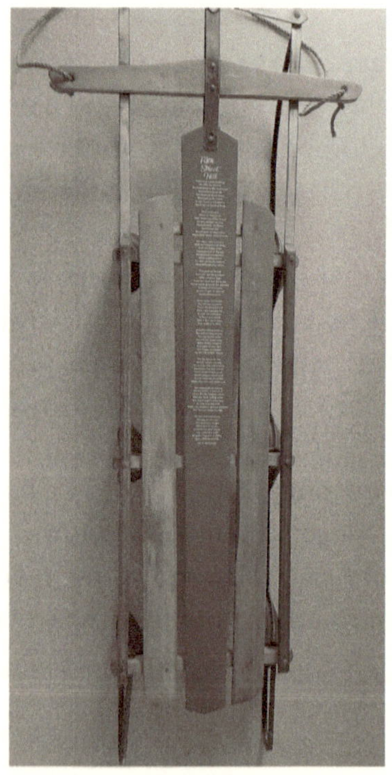

Gift from Perry and Ann Countryman

Growing up in the small town of Snohomish, Washington in the 1930's and '40's, I had the advantage that goes with being in a protective environment - surrounded by wonderful neighbors, great teachers, virtually no criminal activity, loving parents, and a God of unlimited grace. Norman Rockwell would have felt right at home.

The Growing Years

The young boy was born in a town his size:
Small, but nevertheless the eyes
Of all who would know of this valley green
Had reason to long for this peaceful scene
Where life and death, and the years in between
Would allow for a young boy to grow.

He lived on a street lined with Chestnut trees
Where each Autumn produced a parade of leaves,
When gathered by young and old hands where they fell,
Once burning, produced the most marvelous smell
Amid laughter at stories his neighbors would tell.
While the lad would continue to grow.

His young life was full of such wonderful things
That all the adventure of Summertime brings.
Then Winter; the snow and the ice-covered lake.
The cinnamon rolls that his grandma would bake,
Though more than the little boy's stomach could take
Helped the lad to continue to grow.

He grew through the years of the 2nd World War,
To the day there would come from a knock on the door,
The terrible news that his brother was killed
While serving his country; 'twas God who had willed
That this life of such promise should now be stilled.
But the lad; he continued to grow.

The years of a youth are a learning time
Full of change that produces a yearning time.
How lightly are taken the ones more wise
Who were born and remained in a town of this size,
When a curious world waits just beyond the rise
For a boy in a hurry to grow.

Within the days that are marked by man
A time would arrive when the Lord did plan
That the youth depart from his place of birth
To discover in life those things of worth
Wherever he traveled throughout the earth.
So the lad might continue to grow.

He grew into manhood, no longer the lad
With freedom to do all the things that he had.
He married, and fathered a family of five
Of the grandest of children a man could derive
With the love of a woman who brought him alive.
And the man; he continued to grow.

The years slipped away as they always do.
The man now watched as his own children grew
To go off one by one in the world to find
A place of their own where the streets were lined
With the Chestnut trees that had been so kind
To the lad as he had time to grow.

Then the day would arrive when the man returned
To the town where the Chestnut leaves had burned
To stand once more in the memories
Of a time that was filled with a summer breeze,
And a snow-covered hill that was sure to please
Any lad as he had time to grow.

The town had now changed; more people had come.
New trees had to grow, while others succumbed
To the test of old age like all living things.
So, the man also changed, but the change would bring
A new interest in life, like the rebirth in Spring.
When all good things continue to grow.

Oh Lord! Is it him you're now coming to get?
There are so many things that he hasn't done, yet.
Is it possible he might still have a few years
Just to savor the memories, and wipe away tears
Full of joy in his spirit thru born again ears?
And the man might continue to grow.

(Ecclesiastes 1:1-4)

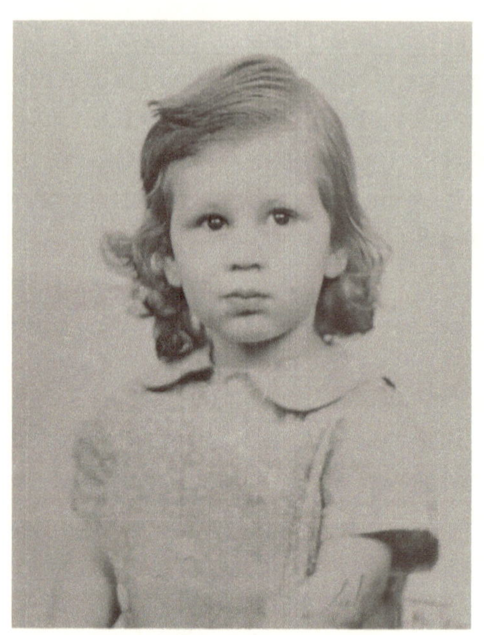

The very young lad

A ferryboat Summertime adventure with
sisters Mary and Nancy (1947)

Me and the girl that knocked my socks off

...and left our kiddos barefoot

The young kiddos
Mark, Garry, Kevin, Tim, Jennifer

... and the not-so-young kiddos
Jennifer, Tim, Garry, Kevin, Mark

Part 2
NATURE

Heron on Clam Rock
"I am the boss of this rock."

Deer seen me-an-deer-ing at the cabin
on San Juan Island

From one foxy lady to another

Flights have been cancelled due to high winds

About George

When I was in 6th grade George followed me home.
Now, George was a kitten, and this is a poem
   – <u>About George.</u>
I asked, "Mom, can I keep him"? At first, she said, "No".
But I was persistent and wouldn't let go.

See, she was reluctant, recalling the past;
The times that my promises just didn't last.
It took some persuasion and twisting her arm,
But while I was at it, I turned on the charm.

I promised to feed him and take special care
To clean any messes and comb shedding hair.
She finally relented and gave me some time
To show that my promise was not just a line.

Now, George was the first pet that I ever had,
And I was determined to make my mom glad
   – <u>About George</u>.
I bought a flea collar that George wouldn't wear.
I thought it might help him, but George didn't care.

Now, George could act feisty, yet, more often tame.
And George didn't always remember his name.
I'd call him and call him. I felt really dumb.
I knew he could hear, but he just wouldn't come.

But bring on the catnip, or bring out the food,
And George let you know he was in a good mood.
He'd lay on his back and roll this way and that.
He'd chase after things at the drop of a hat.

He slept on the couch, and he slept on my bed.
He slept 'till he thought it was time to be fed.
Then, when I left for college my mom fed the cat.
She said it was fine, only problem was that

Between food and sleeping George put on the weight.
He'd take his catnap, then he'd go clean his plate.
He's no longer with us; it all took its toll.
His bed is now empty and so is his bowl.

Oh, please do be careful how much your cat's fed.
And don't share with mother this poem you just read
  – <u>About George.</u>

My neighbor, Jim Holloman, George and me

Me and George (on right)

*I think my enjoyment in beach combing for agates was fostered
by my mom and dad who would frequent Agate Beach among
other beaches on the Northern coast of Oregon when I was
fairly young. Dad would sometimes walk ahead of Mom and
drop agates he had found so Mom would find them and stay on
the beach longer.*

Agates

Where is the sun, Lord? I wish it were here.
We surely could use it this time of the year.
When the sun isn't shining it makes it so hard
To find any agates in nature's backyard.

While looking for agates, bent over in two
I'm kept in the shape of an upside-down U.
Some folks think I'm crazy for spending my hours
With nose to the pebbles instead of the flowers.

But I search the beaches, and minus the sun
It's making it work when it ought to be fun.
I guess all my efforts are going for naught.
For while both eyes are bulging ...

My pockets are not.

** Come out, come out, wherever you are **

They're called "Sneaker Waves" for a reason

Mark and Kevin try their luck

Garry leaves no rock unturned

Ruth appears very confident...and relaxed

The elusive prize!

Aurora Borealis

I remember the night of the Northern Lights
 As they shimmered across the skies.
It was magical there in the Winter air,
 And I couldn't believe my eyes.

I had never seen anything else before
 That could even come close to this;
Like a once in a lifetime happening
 That one couldn't afford to miss.

I stood transfixed and could hardly breathe,
 Yet, I wanted to shout for joy
As they lit up the sky like the 4th of July
 For a very excited young boy.

I called to my family and neighbors, alike,
 "Come and see this unusual sky!"
I wanted them all in due time to recall
 That this night was a feast for the eye.

You could almost hear music perform for its dance
 As it slowly began to fade.
Then crescendo again as it started to send
 Out a pattern that heaven had made.

I stood there so long with my head turned up wrong
    That my neck felt like breaking in two,
So, I lay on my back and there followed its track
    From a now horizontal view.

At the age of thirteen there's no doubt I had seen
    One of nature's remarkable sights.
And if fortune should smile once again on me, I'll
    See the night full of Northern Lights.

Amazing –

- sight to behold

Cat Chat

What meanest thou by that "Meow"?
Is it time to go outside?
Do you want some food; is it just a mood,
Or can't you yet decide?

What meanest you by that "Mew"?
Did you lose your favorite socks?
Is your fur all wet; did someone forget
To refill your litter box?

What meanest him with Cheshire grin?
Does he dream of battles won?
When his whiskers twitch does he have an itch,
Or grinning just for fun?

What meanest her by that loud purr?
Is her highness represented
By the fact she'll stay on the couch all day
And be purr-fectly contented?

Now cats have many things to say
And many things to "Mew".
It's just that puss com("mew")nicates
From a different point of "Miew".

Ruth observing Daphne's Cheshire grin

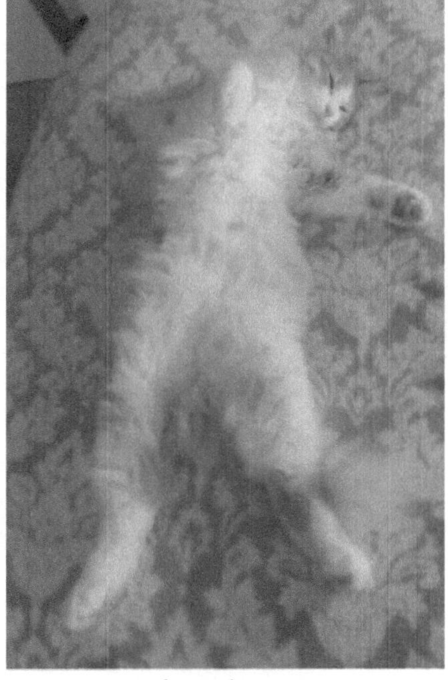

Daphne dreaming

The Pesky Fly

The day we hiked the Mendenhall
Was a warm day in July.
Old Sol was out to welcome us
In the vast Alaskan sky.

We studied the map and followed the signs;
We, being my wife and I.
With no idea that just up ahead
Awaited the pesky fly.

We walked the trail at a steady pace
As it slowly began to rise.
Stopped now and then to enjoy the view,
And to rest against our thighs.

On one such stop halfway to the top
I uttered a muffled cry
As the first alarm from a bite on my arm,
I encountered the pesky fly.

I flailed away at this foreign prey,
Having never been bit before
By a Juneau fly on a trail where I
Was the object of all-out war.

But to no avail; moving up the trail,
No matter how hard we try,
We couldn't evade in sun or in shade
The infamous pesky fly.

We stopped to view the emerald hue;
The glacier far below,
But now the awe of glacial thaw
Had somehow lost its glow.

 For though attained, our goal had gained
A jaundiced point of view.
What should have been fun in the Juneau sun
Had become my Waterloo.

Now, many a trail we've hiked before,
And many we'll hike again,
But low on the scale is the Juneau trail
That separates boys from men.

Should you heed the call of the Mendenhall
And desire its heights to ply,
It's twenty to one that before you're done
You will battle the pesky fly.

The Mendenhall Glacier, Alaska

Ruth before the fly arrived

Autumn Performs

The colors leap from tree to tree
    As Autumn takes the stage.
The yellows perform brilliantly
    And red is all the rage.
It's really quite delightful
    How the leaves improve with age
When it's Autumn
    And the curtain is ascending.

The comedy of Autumn
    Is the laughing Cottonwood.
The drama is the Sumac
    With its bold red riding hood.
The music of the Maples
    Stirs a melancholy mood
When it's Autumn
    And the show is just beginning.

The Evergreens behind the scenes
    Play straight men to the clowns
Who dress themselves as natures' elves
    In multicolored gowns.
Then dance across the countryside
    And march into the towns
When it's Autumn
    And the scene is ever changing.

Then all too soon the Autumn moon
    Will curl up in a ball,
While Winter, Spring, and Summer come
    To make their curtain call.
'Til once again the writer's pen
    Creates more 'Fall-deral'
Known as Autumn,
    Which we find so entertaining.

Autumn in Snohomish, Wa

The San Juan Rabbits

The San Juan rabbits exercise
   In a most unusual way.
They don't have gyms for hers and hims
   To use throughout the day.
They must rely on things they find
   Like pipe called PVC
That moves clean water over land
   And underground dirt free.

The rabbits start their exercise
   At 6:00 P.M. or so.
You'd see them on the PVC
   A 'swinging to and fro.
But being they're so 'skitterish'
   it's hard to catch their act.
Yet, once I happened on the scene
   At Heights of Hannah Tract.

The evening sun had just begun
   To sink low in the West,
When rabbits gathered at the pipe
   To see who swung the best.

They lined up very orderly
    As each would wait their time
To grab hold of the PVC
    And work up to their prime.

At first, they did some pull-ups
    Just to loosen up their joints.
Then moved into their best routine
    To earn the highest points.
The winner of the day's event
    Would garner much applause,
As rabbits from surrounding tracts
    High-fived each other's paws.

And then, of course, they all would feast
    And sleep; the Buck and Doe.
It's really no surprise to see
    The population grow.
Through exercise and nourishment
    The combination breeds
More healthy little rabbits here
    Than San Juan Island needs.

"You ain't seen nothin', yet!"

*While owners and operators of THE TIDES INN (motel) in
Port Townsend, Washington, we had two female cats that each
gave birth to a litter almost at the same time. These mama cats
were, of course, very protective of their offspring. We were able
to give some of the kittens to our guests when they checked out.
This poem, however, is mostly fictitious.*

Motel Cats

Two cats were making plans one night;
    Their strategy to use.
A dog was seen meandering
    While 'reading evening news'.
The felines read between the lines,
    They knew what they must do.
The dog had taken residence
    In unit twenty-two.

These motel cats had given birth
    A couple weeks before;
An even dozen twixt the two
    Upon the family floor.
Now their protective instincts
    Wouldn't stand for any 'cur
Moving 'bout in the vicinity
    Of where their offspring were.

Their strategy was simple.
    'Let the mangy little mutt
Stick its nose outside that doorway
    And he'd wish it had stayed shut'.
So, they took up guard outside the yard
    Of unit twenty-two,
And there they waited patiently
    For his A.M. debut.

The hour drew close to seven;
    Most the guests were sleeping still,
When the dog made his appearance,
    And they moved in for the kill.
The battle lasted moments,
    But the clash did ricochet
As I woke from sleeping soundly
    From the bed in which I lay.

As I groped to find my clothing,
    While yet stumbling to the door
I realized through sleepy eyes
    I should have put on more.
But time seemed of the essence
    As I rushed to find the source,
And in my haste below the waist
    I wore but boxer shorts.

At last I reached the battleground,
    But all that met my eyes
Were two victorious mothers there
    Beneath the breaking skies.
They had the look of innocence
    While smoothing down their fur,
And smugly walking up the path
    They each began to purr.

We didn't hear the end of that
    For many and a day,
As guests rehashed the story
    Of the tabby and the gray.
And some strange fella running
    Towards the scene that early dawn
So thinly clad in shorts of plaid
    Across the dewy lawn.

The owner of the injured dog
    Was not a happy guest.
Her Dandie Dinmont Terrier
    Had come out second best.
But dog survived, the bill arrived,
    The vet took seven stitches.
The cats are pregnant once again.
    I still sleep in my britches.

Our Tides Inn Motel

Blackie (above) and Pretty Girl (below)

"Our motel, our rules"

Yachats has been a favorite destination for our family for as long as I can remember. The small population, coupled with the variety of coast beach amenities, continues to draw us back each year.

Yachats (Yah-hots)

Have you ever visited Yachats?
　A most wonderful place on the shore.
If you've ever visited Yachats
　You had to go back for some more.

There's mile after mile of blue ocean.
　And smile after smile of blue sky.
The sound of the waves in their crashing
　Is a treat for the ears and the eye.

So, how does someone pronounce Yachats?
　Newcomers may not have a clue.
But those 'in the know' would say <u>Yah-Hots</u>.
　And now 'in the know' includes you.

Now, Yachats is smack in the middle
　Of Oregon State, U. S. A.
The middle, that is, of the coastline.
　Where you'll want to spend more than a day.

So, what's the attraction of Yachats?
　And why do folks like to return?
Well, some search the beaches for agates,
　While still others enjoy 'Devil's Churn'.

The change of the tide reveals blowholes.
    'Thor's Well' is a sight to behold.
It attracts both the young and the grown-ups,
    And somehow just never grows old.

There's a trail that follows the ocean,
    And cliffs with spectacular views.
There's numerous long sandy beaches
    From which you're invited to choose.

You might see gray whales in migration;
    Depending the time of the year.
There's seals and brown pelicans sounding
    A language that some never hear.

I love the sound of the ocean;
    The waves as they crash on the rocks.
The challenge of moving among them
    Protecting your shoes and your socks.

Now, some folks may not think of Yachats
    As a place they had planned to spend time.
Or writing a poem to describe it,
    And trying to make it all rhyme.

But now you know things about Yachats.
    You might say we've opened the door.
So, if you've never visited Yachats
    What on earth then are you waiting for?

Atop Cape Perpetua at Yachats

The always-mesmerizing blowholes

"I think that agate's a keeper"

Need I explain?

Agates – gems of the Oregon Coast

Thar, she blows!
(at Thor's Well)

Oceanfront dining at the Adobe

Staying warm in the brisk salt air celebrating
Ruth's 84th birthday

Part 3
FAITH

Ruth and I spent two weeks in Argentina and Paraguay, South America in 2012 at the invitation of the Kent-based Ukrainian church. They held revival meetings in three locations and purchased supplies to support an orphanage they helped sponsor in the capital of Buenos Aires, Argentina.

Mary Schaefer and myself being welcomed to the Ukrainian church in Buenos Aires.

Ebenezer - Ukrainian men's worship group

Ruth is in her element loving on a young girl
at the orphanage where we brought supplies

Most of the Ukrainian church members from
different locations in Washington state,
Buenos Aires, and the Ukraine that were part
of the missionary team

Choices

A man who loves a challenge
Is a man who's bound to win.
He grits his teeth and dives into the fray.
Each time he hits the canvas
Having took one on the chin
He's on his feet to face another day.

A man who takes no chances
Is a man who's bound to lose.
They'll never put the laurel on his head.
Each time he hits the canvas
He will only have a bruise
And another reason to remain in bed.

Each man makes the decision;
Face the challenge or retreat.
On that his main existence will depend.
He'll either taste of vict'ry;
The alternative – defeat.
His character is molded in the end.

So, choose to face the challenge.
And choose to seek the crown.
Then enter the arena for you see
In doing daily battle,
Though your world be upside down
You're bound to win with God as referee.

(Romans 8:31-33)

The Face of God

I went to church last Sunday night
   And didn't see You there.
I tried so hard to concentrate,
   But all I did was stare.

Each time the door would open
   I had hoped it might be You,
But it was just another face
   To fill another pew.

It seemed so long since last I sensed
   Your presence in that place.
The memory of our meeting there
   Which time cannot erase

Still brings a sense of awe that makes
   My eyes well up with tears
Just thinking how my life was saved,
   And changed throughout the years.

'Twas 50 years ago today
   When first I heard Your voice;
So quiet, yet I understood
   I had to make a choice.

I chose to let You take control
   To make me someone who
Would yield my willful, stubborn heart
   And start my life anew.

For many years I followed You
    And hungered for Your Word.
I couldn't seem to get enough
    Of love You ministered.

But time and busyness creep in
    And cloud priorities.
I spent more time pursuing goals
    Than time spent on my knees.

But You're extremely patient
    And You give sufficient room
For empty hearts to seek
    To reunite the bride and groom.

I realized it wasn't You
    Who seemed to disappear,
But this lost soul that took control
    And didn't want to hear.

You never really left at all;
    'Twas I that couldn't see
You seated there among Your flock
    Where You would always be.

Oh, may I never doubt again
    That You are in that place.
I only have to see Your love
    In each and every face.

(2nd Chronicles 7:14-16)

Jesus Walked (The Feet of Jesus)

Jesus walked with His disciples,
   And He walked with Pharisees.
Jesus walked upon the mountain,
   And He walked upon the sea.

Jesus walked among all peoples
   As He shared the Word of God,
Teaching all to love each other
   Where 'er their feet may trod.

Jesus walked to Caesarea,
   And He walked to Bethany.
Jesus walked throughout Capernaum,
   And the shores of Galilee.

Mary washed the feet of Jesus,
   And she dried them with her hair.
Then she bathed them with her perfume,
   Causing everyone to stare.

These were feet that carried Jesus
   To the tomb where Lazarus lay.
Calling forth the sister's brother,
   Lazarus came without delay.

Martha worked to prepare dinner.
   Mary sat at Jesus` feet.
Martha wanted her to help her.
   Mary didn't want to eat.

Jesus prayed and walked the garden
    That was called Gethsemane.
When the soldiers came to grab Him,
    The disciples chose to flee.

Jesus walked the Delarosa
    On the way to Calvary
Where His feet were nailed to timber,
    Crucified for you and me.

He arose just three days later.
    Then He walked right out of Hell,
And de(feet)ed sin forever.
    Oh, there's so much more to tell.

As He walked with sad disciples
    To Emmaus late that night,
They discovered it was Jesus
    As He disappeared from sight.

He walked right through a closed door
    To show Thomas hands and side.
Then ascended to the Father
    To await His coming bride.

Until then let's walk as He did,
    Showing love to all we meet,
Then as saints we'll kneel before Him
    Laying crowns at Jesus' feet.

(Isaiah 52:7 / Romans 10:15)

This poem has hints of my years teaching youths and adults in the public schools and commercial school how to drive a motor vehicle.

The Journey

As we journey through this lifetime
There are many roads to travel.
Some we choose, and some are chosen;
Some are paved, and some are gravel.

Some are strewn with ruts and potholes;
Some with gold and untold wealth.
Yet, there's detours and there's exits
When there's problems with your health.

When the unexpected happens
And we lose sight of our goal,
Out of nowhere comes our Savior
Helping us regain control.

Now our Father sees the hazards,
And He has the right-of-way.
So, He'll steer us safely through them
When we let Him have His say.

So, "Listen to your Father".
He designed us after all
For His Holy Spirit power
Since we first began to crawl.

Oh, there'll still be times we're upset
By the way that others drive.
By roads that lead to nowhere,
Wondering how we will survive.

But when the road gets bumpy,
Or the body needs repair
Keep the "Manual" close and open.
Take it to the Lord in prayer.

(Proverbs 3:6 / Isaiah 30:19-21)

One of many journeys from Santa Rosa, Ca
to Snohomish, Wa
"Are we there, yet?"

The Prisoner

The smile has left his face, Lord,
And there's no life in his eyes.
There's defeat in his expression
Where there used to be surprise.

His laugh, once so engaging
Has been silenced like a door
That's been closed to all that love him,
And seems locked forevermore.

His smile once used to light
The darkest corner of a room.
But now he lives in darkness
Like a prisoner in a tomb.

If we only had the key, Lord,
To unlock what's deep inside.
Now we turn to You for answers
Failing everything we've tried.

Dear God, we know You love him,
And can set the captive free.
So, we thank You now for doing
What we all would love to see.

My Brother; My Hero

In our family Ken was alpha;
    Number one son on the scene.
And before I was omega
    Were two sisters in between.

Now, alpha and omega
    Were at least twelve years apart
Which really made it hard to hitch
    His horse up to my cart.

That dozen years between us
    Made it difficult to know
Just how special my big brother was
    So many years ago.

Story has it there was nothing
    That this big guy couldn't do.
Playing basketball, and french horn,
    Acting, just to name a few.

He then enrolled in college
    Just as World War II began,
So, the next year he enlisted;
    Overnight became a man.

Now, the Army needed Kenneth
    As they fought from Normandy
Through the country, towns, and cities
    To the gates of Germany.

February 22nd,
   1945, would be
The last day for my big brother
   To help set French people free.

That night he volunteered to help
   Locate where snipers lay
So his buddies might be safer
   As they fought another day.

They said it happened quickly;
   In the blinking of an eye.
He was with them, then he wasn't,
   As they saw their buddy die.

The Purple Heart, Bronze, and Silver Star
   He earned while in the war,
But his Savior Jesus Christ
   Awarded life forevermore.

Just like our Lord and Savior
   Gave His life that we might live,
So, my brother at age twenty-two
   Gave all he had to give.

Now, Kenneth is my hero
   For he freely gave his all
For his family, school, and country
   When he answered to the call.

One day we'll greet each other
    Where in eternity we'll spend.
The alpha and omega;
    The beginning and the end.

Staff Sgt. Kenneth C. McCready

Kenneth C. McCready's Purple Heart

Ken and sister Mary (1942)

I wrote the first three verses of this song back around 1953 before I knew Jesus. In 2020 I made a few changes and added the three verses at the end.

Kingdom Come (Song)

When we leave this troubled world
And a new life is unfurled
There will be a great reunion in the sky.
All the old folks with their gray hair
Will be more than glad to stay there
'Cause the cost of livin' won't be near as high.

Now, the girls with all their make-up
Will be happy when they wake up
'Cause there won't be any 'war paint' on a cloud.
All the colors shine forever,
So, when our Father pulls that lever
There's a rainbow round the world just like He vowed.

And, the boys who play them guitars
Will no longer smoke their cigars,
But will sing the songs of glory and of praise.
They'll be shoutin' "Hallelujah"
To the God who'll never fool 'ya.
He's the One the Bible calls 'Ancient of Days'.

(Chorus)
Lord, won't You take my soul to Heaven.
Lord, I pray to see the land above.
Lord, let me live within Your Kingdom,
And dwell in the sunshine of Your love.

Lord, my life's been far from pretty,
And my tongue may not be witty,
But I know my name's been written in Your 'Book'.
So, I'm lookin' up to glory
'Cause I've read the written story,
And I know the blood You shed was what it took.

Friend, if you want to be included,
Then regardless of what you did,
You can ask the Lord to wash away the past.
Take the promise that is offered
From the 'Book' that He has authored,
And you'll live a life of joy and peace at last.

As I write this final chapter
To the folks who may come after,
I've been thinking that this song is far too long.
So, forgive me if my preaching
Doesn't help you in your seeking
For the One who taught us all what's right and wrong.

(Chorus)

Laughter

Laughter is medicine, scriptures declare:
It's health to the bones and the spirit.
When something is humorous - story or joke,
You're hooked from the moment you hear it.

A laugh is contagious; it starts with a smile,
But that's usually just the beginning.
What follows then may be a chuckle or snort,
And the next thing you know you'll be grinning.

You may be in church or a hospital bed
When out of the blue something funny
Will tickle you so that you can't let it go
'Till you shake with an ache in your tummy.

Whether wealthy or poor there is one thing for sure,
When you're laughing it makes your heart lighter.
A room full of gloom is a portent of doom,
But the moment you're laughing it's brighter.

When the rent's overdue and it's mulligan stew
Now the third day for dinner you're having,
Just be thankful you've got something left in the pot.
Let that thought fill your belly with laughing.

So, here's to the woman and here's to the man
Who may stand on the brink of disaster.
Though you seemingly have nothing else you can give,
Share with someone the gift of your laughter.

(Proverbs 17:22 / Psalm 126:2)

"Make 'em laugh, make 'em laugh!"

Don't take life too seriously

Heather, Roberta and Margie
"Alright, what's so funny?"

Jennifer loving Fabiola to death

"You've got to be kidding me!"

"Seriously? Are you related to these people?!"

I had the privilege of being the principal of a new Christian school in Port Townsend, Washington for 7 years, (1978 - 85). It was both a joy and a challenge working with several wonderful Christian men and women who sacrificed much time and energy as we learned together what we prayed was blessing God and the students. A tribute to Pastor Dennis, who went the extra mile to help get us on track and keep us there through some rather turbulent but rewarding times.

Cornerstone

Somebody once suggested that
   We start a Christian school.
I said, "Don't look at me, my friend.
   I ain't nobody's fool."
But a fella named Rick Osborn
   Had a most convincing way.
And he stated quite succinctly,
   "Son, I think you'd better pray."

"Let me tell you something, fella,
   Now before you get much older.
You'll never hit the baseball
   With the bat left on your shoulder.
So, take a swing at anything
   That winds up in your strike zone.
Then flip your bat and tip your hat
   While rounding 3rd to head home."

Well, the time we had was little,
    And the money almost nil,
But it's funny how they multiply
    When moving in God's will.
Pastor Dennis gave the 'go-ahead';
    The board fell right in line.
Some thought that we were foolish;
    Others said, "you're do'in fine."

Now, the Hickenbottom family
    Had a daycare on the rise.
They said, "There's always room for more,
    We'll make it twice the size."
So, the work began in earnest
    With the help of volunteers.
But even so, the work was slow
    As opening day drew near.

The Baptist church on Lawrence
    Offered us their lower floor.
Satan once again was beaten
    Like so many times before.
We built four dozen 'offices'
    Down at ol' Noah's Ark.
The time they found for doing that
    Was mostly after dark.

We opened right on schedule,
    All the 'offices' were filled.
And once a month our Penny
    Saw the parents all got billed.
We chose the name of Cornerstone;
    It had a stable sound.
We wanted our foundation
    To be built on solid ground.

We had a staff that worked long hours
    For very little pay.
That didn't seem to bother them,
    "We're serving God", they'd say.
It wasn't always easy
    As you'd probably surmise,
But saw what God was doing daily
    Right before our eyes.

Our Lord was always faithful,
    And He never let us down.
Each time we faced a crisis,
    We would grab hold of His gown.
You often wonder what became
    Of each and every soul
That God entrusted to our care
    With Heaven as His goal.

We had a lot of fun those years
    Of trying something new.
You only pray that in some way
    Your efforts will ring true.
That in the end you'll find the trend
    Bore fruit for Christ our Lord.
And hear the words, "Well done, My son"
    And see them all on board.

His banner over us is Love.

Cornerstone Christian Academy float in
Port Townsend Rhododendron parade.

Cornerstone students and staff (1981)

Cornerstone girls volleyball team

Cornerstone boys basketball team

Part 4
FAMILY

Welcome to Winter (W2W)
at Eric and Corinne Hill's home - 2009

My 75th birthday - 2010

Mary's 90-year birthday celebration – 2016

McCready BBQ
Fort Worden/Port Townsend – 2018

Aunt Clara (Krit)

Aunt Clara Mae was thirty
   When she married Uncle Nim.
She knew just what she wanted
   When she set her sights on him.

She wanted Nim for better
   And she wanted Nim for worse.
At the time he was a soldier
   And Aunt Clara was a nurse.

She saw Nim on a street in France
   In nineteen seventeen,
So handsome in his uniform
   Approaching the canteen.

She coyly dropped her hanky
   As the soldier reached her side.
He gallantly retrieved it
   And took Clara as his bride.

Now Clara was determined
    At the end of World War One
To see her husband prosper;
    Not to let him be outdone.

Their early years were busy;
    Climb the ladder of success.
First, a move to San Francisco
    With a Broadway Street address.

Nim started at the bottom,
    But with gradual ascent,
With an advertising firm
    He soon became vice-president.

But, back to Clara Kyrage,
    That's her maiden name, you see;
This coy White Russian lady
    With a first-class pedigree.

She cooked the finest dinners
    When she had a reason to.
Then sell her recipes to you
    To make a buck or two.

A favorite expression
    You would often hear her say,
Was, "ye gods", when something happened
    That would cause her much dismay.

She shopped at Saks and Macy's
    When she needed something new.
But she visited the Goodwill
    When she bought a gift for you.

Her voice was very raspy;
    Her appearance always "smart".
Though at times she could offend you,
    She could also win your heart.

Aunt Clara was a Catholic,
    And did faithfully attend
To light her many candles
    That petitions might ascend.

Nim used a favorite nickname;
    As he called Aunt Clara, "Krit".
I don't know just what the name meant,
    But he used it quite a bit.

When Nim died, Clara faltered;
    Things would never be the same.
They had a childless marriage;
    None to carry on the name.

Now Clara came to visit us
    A few days at a time.
She'd bring sardines and crackers
    With a little gin and lime.

She had a fear of felines
    That she carried from the womb.
If our cat made an appearance
    She'd run screaming from the room.

By nine it was her bedtime,
    But she wanted company.
So, she donned her eye protectors
    And retired with Timothy.

The youngest of four brothers,
    Tim would never choose to stay.
So, when Clara fell asleep
    Then he could make his getaway.

Now, Aunt Clara was a classic;
    One you never quite forget.
This strange White Russian lady
    That my Uncle Nim called, "Krit".

Aunt Clara "Krit"

*No one can recall exactly how these words came about, but it
became an endearment somehow for my sister, Nancy, and
myself to use when referring to my sister Mary, who was nine
years older than me.*

Booder Mouse

"Booder Mouses Manners Cuckoo"
Now, what kind of name is that?
And yet somehow that very name
Was hung on Mary Pat.

Mary Pat's my oldest sister
And she doesn't look at all
Like a mouse who has no manners,
Or a Cuckoo on the wall.

And where the "Booder" came from
I just haven't got a clue.
I suppose just like the others
It evolved out of the blue.

The name is just a montage
Of four words unrelated.
And stringing them together
Was like nonsense orchestrated.

We called her "Booder Mouse" for short.
'Twas easier that way
Than spouting all the other words
Like some strange popinjay.

She seems to lead a normal life
Despite the name of "Booder";
Now living up in Canada
Somewhere in North Vancouver.

Of course her friends are most kind;
Never mentioning her name,
But secretly admire this
Handicap she overcame.

So, if you hear someone call
"Booder Mouses Manners Cuckoo"
They're not calling to a rodent
Or a wayward cockatoo (too).

Somebody's calling Mary,
And she'll answer, foe or friend,
To the name already mentioned
Or this poem would have no end.

Sister Mary with daughters Krista and Kathy –
1949

Mary "Booder Mouses Manners Cuckoo"

Fabiola Montoya, a foreign exchange student from Chihuahua, Mexico, spent her senior year in high school with us back in 1990 when we lived in Kent, Washington. She was a very pleasant addition to the family, and still much loved by all.

Fabiola

Her name is Fabiola;
    She arrived nine months ago;
A brown-eyed senorita
    From Chihuahua, Mexico.
Our meeting I'll remember
    For as long as I shall live,
For in those precious moments
    She gave all she had to give.

Her face was full of tenderness,
    And long we did embrace
As tears flowed ever freely
    In that crowded greeting place.
She didn't speak 'the English'
    Like she may have wanted to,
But spoke another language
    That was known to precious few.

Her parents had entrusted
    Their 'delight' for us to share
Knowing full well that the God of love
    Would keep her in His care.
And we two dads; the giving one,
    And me, the waiting host
Experienced emotions deep;
    God knows who struggled most.

For one would have to say adios,
    And wait for her return.
The other try to fill the shoes
    For one her heart would yearn.
The shoe's now on the other foot
    As we bid her goodbye,
And once again the airport
    Is a place to laugh and cry.

While she was here, she studied hard,
    And still had time for fun.
We traveled many places
    Just to show her Washington.
She traveled north to Canada;
    Victoria, B.C.
She traveled east to Leavenworth,
    Which looks like Germany.

She saw the whales in Puget Sound;
    The deer at Mt. Rainier.
She saw a lot of movies
    Where 'we had to shed a tear'.
She joined us Christmas caroling;
    She paddled a canoe.
She did the square dance with her friends,
    And visited the zoo.

We celebrated birthdays
    At Azteca Restaurant.
She went to the Puyallup Fair,
    And rode an elephant.
She got her driver's license
    When she once learned how to stop.
Went up the ol' Space Needle;
    Ate a dinner at the top.

She struggled through the rainy days
    Of which there were a lot.
She tried her luck at fishing;
    Didn't eat the fish she caught.
She tried her hand at drawing,
    And she sewed a pair of 'chorts'.
She often got to wear them
    As she played a lot of sports.

She painted trim within the house
    That Dave and Jenny bought.
At Longacres she bet two bucks
    To watch the horses trot.
She took a lot of teasing,
    And created quite a flap
The night she spilled a glass
    Of ice-cold water in her lap.

She did a lot of other things;
    I've only mentioned some,
And it would take too long to mention
    Each and every one.
But why she never loved our cat
    I never understood,
Especially when poor Fluffy
    Always tried to be so good.

It seems like only yesterday
    We welcomed to our home
This foreign exchange student
    Who became one of our own.
And when one day in Mexico
    We see you, lovely daughter,
We want to meet your family,
    But we'll skip the drinking water.

Fabiola Montoya and Kevin

Fabiola at bat in her "chorts"

A Letter to Jennifer

My Dearest Daughter, Jennifer,
  Your mother thought that I
Should write a letter to you,
  But when I'd start, I'd cry.
I cried when you were born, you know.
  They say that's not for men.
And now you're getting married
  And I'm crying once again.

Now all these tears are happiness;
  I've been so very blessed
To have you as a daughter,
  And then this year as a guest.
Well, be that as it may,
  The whole idea of this poem
Is to tell you that I love you
  While away or here at home.

Through all the years of growing;
  Through the good times and the bad,
You've been a source of joy to me;
  The joy of being 'Dad'.
A new adventure waits for you;
  It's full of the unknown.
But we have confidence
  That you and Dave are not alone.

For, Jesus Christ will be your guest,
    And not for just a year.
He's with you always in your joy,
    And times you shed a tear.
One day our phone will ring,
    And Ruth will ask me who has called her.
I'll start to say, "It's Jen",
    Then catch myself; "It's Mrs. Alder".

Your Loving Dad,

Trying to keep my composure
with such a beautiful bride

I wrote this poem in 2020 about my wife, Ruth. I hope people don't misunderstand and think that I'm stuck <u>with</u> Ruth. I've been stuck <u>on</u> the girl (married) for over 65 years.

Stuck On You

How come I was so lucky
   That I got stuck on you?
Some say it wasn't luck at all,
   It was the brand of glue.

There must be glue in Heaven then
   'Cause I prayed 'til I found
A girl so true that just like glue
   She had to stick around.

I never did like sticky stuff
   But what's a guy to do?
I had to change my mind on that
   When I got stuck on you.

You're all the things that I could want
   But didn't have a clue
That God was mixing up a batch
   Of Heaven's brand of glue.

I know that I'm the lucky one
   And folks would say that's true
And so I say I thank the day
   That I got stuck on you.

Heavenly glue

Still sticky after all these years

Little Pete (The Name Game)

My father's name was Irving;
   Born in 1896.
Now oft' times there is a story
   'Bout a name a parent picks.
If that's so I never heard it,
   And it seems I'm not alone.
How his mom and dad chose Irving
   Is a story that's unknown.

Never thought too much about it,
   But when dad and friends would meet
They would never call him Irving,
   But referred to him as 'Pete'.
His middle name was Spencer
   So that didn't help explain
Why so many people knew him
   By a very different name.

As the years passed Dad was active
   In our small town as I grew.
School board member; volunteering;
   And he owned a business too.
Then one year he had a boat built,
   And its length just eighteen feet.
Didn't want to call it Irving
   So we named it "Little Pete".

It had a smaller dinghy
    That was towed behind the boat
So, if "Little Pete" had trouble
    It might keep us all afloat.
We called the dinghy "Re-Pete"
    To let everybody know
That where "Little Pete" would travel
    There would be a "Re-Pete" show.

Now when Dad's health was declining
    His doctor thought it smart
To spend some time away from work
    To be kind to his heart.
They found a little cabin
    We could rent right on the beach.
"Little Pete" remained at anchor
    But was always within reach.

Now my mother took to fishing
    Which she'd never done before.
So, while I was rowing "Re-Pete"
    She was catching fish galore.
She caught at least a dozen
    By the time I rowed back in.
When my dad looked in the dinghy,
    Wow, you should have seen his grin.

A stranger walking by said,
    "Take those fish in right away.
You can only catch so many fish
    On any given day".
We followed his advice and got them
    Cleaned and in the freezer.
'Pete' just smiled at all mom's busyness,
    But how he loved to tease her.

The day would come when it was time
    For "Little Pete" to leave us.
It happened not too long
    Before Dad went to be with Jesus.
A neighbor bought our "Little Pete",
    But "Re-Pete" wasn't needed.
The little dinghy now at rest
    And not to be 'Re-Peted'.

The day will come when Dad will yet
    Receive another name.
The last; the best; bestowed by One
    Whose Name's above all names.
And 'Pete' won't need a boat to float:
    He might just walk on water.
And so impress my mom that she'll
    Be glad the day he 'caught' her.

Irving "Pete" McCready

Maiden voyage of "Little Pete"

"Little Pete" headed for Everett docks

A motley crew in "Re-Pete"

Twins

Twins begins with two that wins
   The hearts of those who know them.
Each special in their separate ways,
   Yet God knew how to grow them.
To make them look so much alike
   It's hard for some to tell
The difference between Mel and Rach
   When Rach looks just like Mel.

Now Melanie and Rachel
   Are the product of what seems
Is God's own sense of humor
   As He takes the parents genes,
And fusses in His workshop
   'Til He's got just what He's after;
Two little girls with golden curls
   And faces full of laughter.

They'll break some fellas heart one day;
   Right now they're having fun,
Just keeping Grandpa guessing
   If there's two or only one.
He thinks he's seeing double
   When they both pop into view.
While others find it easy,
   Gramps just doesn't have a clue.

It doesn't really matter;
    He's just tickled they exist.
When each one comes to kiss him
    How could any gramp' resist.
He's learned to keep his mouth shut;
    Love the kiss and never tell
That he's still got no idea
    Which is Rach and which is Mel.

Melanie and Rachel -or- Rachel and Melanie

The High Flopping MacC's

♌ ♌ ♌ ♌

While most folks have heard of the term jumping jacks,
How many have heard of the high jumping MacC's?
If you followed the track team at Port Townsend High
In the mid-to-late 70's you'd understand why.

Now, how they got started I really can't say,
But once they got going they jumped every day.
All three began jumping when still fairly young.
It seemed they were playing and just having fun.

But wait, now I'm getting ahead of my poem.
Seems the Summer Olympics were on in our home.
And while watching on TV the high jump event
Saw this guy clear the bar with his body so bent

That unlike other jumpers with legs over first
This fella was clever, or else he was worst.
He ran at the bar, twisted 'round, gave a leap.
First his head, then his back, then his thighs, last his feet

Sailed over the bar just as slick as you please,
And before you could clap he was up on his knees.
The 'Fosbury Flop' was the name that would stick
Although the name 'flop' really could have been 'kick'.

Who knew that this 'flopping' would take such a hold
That it soon was the style that became good as gold.
Well, the guys took to 'flopping' like gals like to shop,
And once they got started, they just couldn't stop.

Their mother went searching for fragments of foam
That stores were discarding; then bringing it home
She bound them together with burlap and thread;
Enough to protect both their back and their head.

One moment they're running; the next in the air
While clearing the crossbar with inches to spare.
They'd run at that bar as though under attack;
Then twisting and turning they'd land on their back.

They practiced perfecting the Fosbury 'Flop'
'Til they could no longer 'flop' over the top.
They 'flopped' on the field, they 'flopped' in the gym.
They 'flopped' at the track meets to help their team win.

They set a school record, then went on to State
Where they took first and second right out of the gate.
So, Mark, Kevin, Garry, who were high jumping jacks
Would end their careers as the high 'flopping' MacC's.

Garry, Mark, and Kevin - 1976

Getting ready for liftoff

Up, up, and away!
(from bottom to top - Garry, Kevin, Mark)

Jenny's David

&&&&

In her eyes David flies like Peter Pan.
In her eyes David vies to be her man.

In her mind Jenny's blind to David's faults.
In her mind Jenny does the David Waltz.

In her heart David's part of all that's good.
In her heart David says the things he should.

In her thoughts David has a winning smile.
In her thoughts David walks her down the aisle.

In her dreams David built the Taj Mahal.
In her dreams David's at her beckoned call.

In her world Jenny's curled in David's arms.
In her world David's caught in Jenny's charms.

Welcome To Winter (W2W)

A note came in the mail today
    From someone you may know
A most unusual message
    With a closing, "Ho!, Ho!, Ho!"
It said, "W2W
    Is just a month away,
So, here's a picture postcard
    Of the place we're going to stay."

Now, 'W2W'
    Could mean from 'Wall to Wall',
Which matched the 'W2W',
    But made no sense at all.
The other thought that came to mind was,
    This is 'Way too Weird'
Then I recalled the note was from
    The man who's grown a beard.

I should have known that Timothy
    Would find a clever phrase
To get us all to planning
    How we're going to spend our days.
So, 'W2W'
    Is just an acronym
That says 'Welcome to Winter';
    A reminder sent from Tim.

'Twas his idea years ago
    That prior to Christmas Day,
The family gather someplace new
    To eat, and laugh, and play.
Tim always strung some Christmas lights
    To brighten up the place.
With Christmas music playing
    There were smiles on every face.

When we would get together
    There was more than one guitar;
While guessing outside temperatures,
    And candies in the jar.
We each would bring a gift to share,
    And shake the dice to see
Who chose the gift that caught their eye
    Beneath the Christmas tree.

That weekend's always been a treat;
    The memories abound.
'Welcome to Winter' welcomes us
    Each time it comes around.
Yes, Tim's idea sure bore fruit
    Some twenty years ago.
We're still enjoying 'W2W',
    And hoping it might snow.

Nothing beats a log cabin in snow for W2W

Tim tests a new non-caloric silicone-based
kitchen lubricant that creates a surface 500
times more slippery than any cooking oil

Mom wins the coveted candy jar at W2W

Snow angels every year

Part 5
MEMORIES

Last known picture of my family all together

Grandma Greta loved the cabin on San Juan Is

"Take me out to the (Mariners) ballgame!"

And some back porch chillin' at the cabin

Scissors, Comb, and Shears

I lost some hair the other day.
It disappeared the same old way.
A man I've known for fifty years
Applied his scissors, comb, and shears.

We met when I was but a lad;
An introduction from my dad.
I greeted him with childish tears;
The man with scissors, comb, and shears.

'Bout once a month on Saturday
It got to where I'd hear him say,
"It must be time to lower ears",
And use the scissors, comb, and shears.

Through junior high my hair was short
While playing on the hardwood court.
He came to see most all our games,
And knew most all the players' names.

A jolly man, he seemed to know
That hair styles change as young men grow.
To be accepted by my peers,
The hair soon covered both my ears.

We always had a lot to share
While I sat in the barber's chair.
He'd ask if I were college-bound,
And talk of girls went round and round.

A small town barber has a way
Of knowing what goes on each day.
Believes 'bout half of what he hears
While using scissors, comb, and shears.

From boy to man and in between
We two would view the changing scene.
I sure enjoyed his company,
And barbershop philosophy.

One day he'll pack his tools away,
And take a well-earned holiday
He'll find himself an easy chair
And someone else will cut my hair.

Now, fifty years have come and gone
With hair cut short and hair left long.
My black hair now is silver gray
When it gets cut on Saturday.

But Saturdays will never be
The same without his chemistry.
He's left me treasured souvenirs;
The man with scissors, comb, and shears.

Framed and gifted by son Mark

Grandma's House

My grandma's house was always warm;
    Too warm for me, I think.
But cookies in the cookie jar
    And lemonade to drink
Would keep me coming back again
    To visit with her there;
The words of wisdom coming forth
    While rocking in her chair.

A well-read Bible by her side;
    She always had a verse
To help me understand myself
    For better or for worse.
And from her lap a ball of yarn
    Would gradually unwind
To form the most delightful things
    From her creative mind.

The smell of baking filled the air;
    Her pastries were a prize.
Although she seldom measured,
    Scrumptious treats materialized.
Her garden grew most everything
    That one would want to eat.
But when the stove was lit, of course,
    It added to the heat.

Each room was filled with pillowed lace,
    And pictures on the wall
Provoking pleasant memories
    Of times she could recall.
She told me tales of yesteryear
    When she was but a youth
Growing up in Minnesota;
    Not so distant from Duluth.

Where winter storms piled high
    From house to barn, the drifts of snow
Deep enough to tunnel under
    As they traveled to and fro.
I'll venture that's the reason
    For the eighty-two degrees
That the thermostat felt set at,
    So that Grandma wouldn't freeze.

Grandma Shaddie

CHEERS was written in 2003 to help commemorate our class reunion of 1953 from Snohomish High School in Snohomish, Washington.

Cheers For 50 Years

Has it really been 50 years
    Since we let out raucous cheers;
Throwing cap and tassel high into the air?
As we led the celebration
    Of a 12-year education,
Stepping forth into the world we knew not where.

Some would join the U.S. forces.
    Others looked to college courses;
While still others sought employment right away.
Though the road that each would travel
    Might be paved with gold or gravel;
At least we had the choice to go or stay.

That the world was waiting for us
    Was an oft` repeated chorus,
But no matter where we journeyed far or wide,
We would taste the drive-in milkshakes;
    See the faces of our classmates,
And hear the echoes ring for Panther pride.

123

A salute to all our teachers
    Who would often sound like preachers
To be upright, fair, and honest through the years.
Be it Chemistry or Typing
    They would never stand for griping,
And you'd better be respectful to your peers.

While we've done a lot of living;
    Lots of taking; lots of giving,
And these 50 years will be our legacy.
So, each coming generation
    Will enjoy their celebration,
And become the very best that they can be.

Now cheers to you and cheers to me,
    And the golden class of '53.
And raise a toast to those who've gone before.
Though we each could tell our story
    Of the struggles and the glory,
We will cheer Snohomish High forevermore.

Me (in back) singing with the *7 Teens* at a prom

124

Snohomish High School

Snohomish High School Yearbook 1953

*The house that I grew up in had a floor-to-ceiling clock that
stood in a corner of the living room. The story goes that back in
the 1930s a clock salesman couldn't pay his lodging bill at the
end of his stay at the New Brunswick Hotel, which was built
and owned by my grandfather, Dr. Norman McCready, in
Snohomish, Washington. He left the clock in lieu of payment
until he could obtain the resources to clear the tab. He never
did reclaim it and the clock became ours. It was always a
source of pleasure and comfort to me, especially when the
house was void of noise and activity.*

The Grandfather Clock

It stands in the corner so straight and so tall;
Its face near the ceiling; Its back to the wall.
The people that passed hardly noticed at all.
Tick Tock! Tick Tick! Tick a Tock!

For years it was faithful in keeping the time.
You could count on its presence and stature sublime.
Find comfort and peace in the hourly chime.
  Tick Tock! Tick Tick! Tick a Tock!

The pendulum moved like a huge metronome
Marking time and events that took place in the home.
Its elegance fashioned in copper and chrome.
  Tick Tock! Tick Tick! Tick a Tock!

The weeks and months and years passed by.
The hours and minutes and seconds would fly,
But seldom was noticed its soft lullaby.
    Tick Tock! Tick Tick! Tick a Tock!

One day it grew silent from constant neglect,
But the Master of time wasn't through with it, yet.
The pendulum stilled; just a dark silhouette.
    No Tock! No Tick! Tick a Tock!

A subtle reminder; it soon became clear.
The room and the home had lost some of its cheer.
So, the clock was repaired and again one could hear
    Tick Tock! Tick Tick! Tick a Tock!

God teaches us lessons through everyday things.
The tick of a clock and a chime when it rings.
Enjoy every moment, whatever it brings.
    Each Tock! Each Tick! Tick a Tock!

Just think of the stories if we could unlock
The tongue and the voice of that grandfather clock.
No! It's probably best that we can't hear it - Talk.
    Just Tock! Just Tick! Tick a Tock!

Mary, Mom, Nancy, and
2 grandfathers

Same clock; different time and place

Papa Played Piano

When Papa played piano
   Heaven turned a deafened ear.
It was the saddest, mournful sound
   That I would ever hear.

When Mama played piano
   All of heaven would rejoice
To hear her sing a joyful song
   In her angelic voice.

While Mama used a hymn book,
   Papa used the human heart.
And when he played it wasn't long
   Before my tears would start.

I usually had to leave the room
   To find a place to cry.
If someone were to ask,
   I wouldn't know the reason why.

I only know the song he played
   Was in a minor key,
And when he started singing
   It somehow affected me.

Now, Mama played the written notes,
    While Papa played by ear.
The difference was when Papa played,
    I always shed a tear.

I loved the music both would play;
    It stirred me deep inside.
When Mama played my heart would sing;
    When Papa played, I cried.

I guess my love of music came
    From both my mom and dad.
Her music that was happy
    And his music that was sad.

They both are now in Heaven
    Where there's music every day.
Mama plays the grand piano,
    But they won't let Papa play.

Irving "Pete" Spencer McCready

Back in 1958 when Ruth and I had few resources, for Christmas we gathered walnuts from a tree growing in the yard of our rental home in Santa Rosa, California, shelled them and wrapped them in Christmas wrapping as presents for our mothers. I wrote this poem to go with that gift. We were not as yet born again at this time in our lives.

The Mystery of Christmas

A Christmas tree, a fireplace,
   With all the stockings hung in place.
A painting cast on moonlit snow.
   A boy, a girl, and mistletoe.

A holy church with windows stained.
   A holly wreath through frosted pane.
A candle red, a candle green,
   A silver bell; all these we've seen.

A roasting turkey fills the air
   With thoughts of goodies yet to share.
A berry, pumpkin, mincemeat pie,
   And Christmas cookies catch your eye.

The fragrance of the fir and pine
   Is nature's gift at Christmas time.
The scent of walnuts being shelled;
   The candied fruit, all these we've smelled.

The Christmas play that's held each year,
    And brings to most a smile and tear.
The girl who sings "O Holy Night".
    The boy who's halo fits too tight.

The parents who would love to tell
    The whispered secrets kept so well.
The songs of Christmas, as before,
    Are sung again from door to door.

"A Christmas Carol" may be read,
    And finished just in time for bed.
While each child dreams it word for word,
    Ah, Silent Night; all these we've heard.

Down thru the years all these we've known;
    The wondrous things with which we've grown.
The treasured tales so often told;
    So priceless to the young and old.

We're told that Santa drives a sleigh
    That somehow never goes astray.
We're told his reindeer number eight,
    And fly for fear of being late.

We know that Jesus came to earth,
    And choose to celebrate His birth
In many ways with gifts and more,
    Regardless if you're rich or poor.

Although this may sound quite absurd,
    There's still a tale that's gone unheard.
Just who's the one behind the light
    That makes our Christmas day so bright?

This mystery now remains no more.
    The person this was written for?
We're filled with joy and love because,
    We know you're Mrs. Santa Claus.

Thanks MOM!
We love you to the North Pole and back!

Mrs. Santa Claus (Greta) between seasons

For Being My Grandmother

For being my Grandma, you've had quite a chore.
You gave birth to mother and she to some more.
And now to the tally which you have begun
We'll add to that number a daughter or son.

With pins, bibs, and bottles, and pink diaper pails
We'll keep growing younger with Grimm's Fairy Tales.
You wrote that you think that your youth is far spent.
You expect I'll agree with the message you sent.

But I've news for a Grandma whose hair may be gray.
You seem to get younger with each passing day.
Oh, I know what you'll tell me; you don't hear so well.
And that hip that was broken each time that you fell.

But your love and your faith which you've given to all
Has made us much stronger so we might not fall.
You mustn't think lightly of things I have said,
They come from my heart, Gram, as well as my head.

You're not just somebody whose chain may be yanked,
But a Godly example that I've never thanked -----
FOR BEING MY GRANDMA.

P.S.

The reason I'm sending this verse in my poem,
Is it's so hard to kiss you while so far from home.

X O X O X

Me and Grandma "Hattie" Shadinger

Ruth and I traveled to Chihuahua, Mexico in 1999 to attend the marriage ceremony for Fabiola Montoya (our foreign exchange student), and Jorge Zambrano. We had a wonderful time visiting and getting to know her parents and family.

The Marquis of Chihuahua

If you ever should visit Chihuahua
There's a family that you ought to meet.
Maria, Ramon, three gals and a guy,
And a Bonnie with four happy feet.

Now, the three senoritas are lovely,
And they each are a special delight.
Their laughter, and singing, and acting
Entertained us far into the night.

The son had a talent for writing
Such beautiful songs that he played
On his Spanish guitar for his Laura,
And he'll sing them for you s'il vous plait.

Maria was always so gracious
Providing for all of our needs.
The food preparation was marvelous
For family and guests that she feeds.

This brings me to Papa Montoya;
The 'Marquis' I've saved to the end.
The grand 'Marquis of Chihuahua',
So named by Enrique, his friend.

To look at this man of distinction;
A man who loves "smelling the wood";
You might think him 'Marquis of Chihuahua',
But a 'Marquis' who's generous and good.

For a king who would open his castle
To Americanos from Kent,
Is a father much loved by his family,
And by all who would enter his tent.

So, here's to the 'King of Chihuahua';
The man who would let his guest drive
Their car through a river of water
And return to his castle alive.

The wedding, and 'grand celebration'
Was a wonderful end to our stay.
And we ask for God's blessings upon them
'Til they come to our casa to play.

Maria and Ramon Montoya

Ruth and me with Jorge and Fabiola
at their wedding in Chihuahua, Mexico

My sister, Mary, and Warren Kalbach purchased the cabin on San Juan Island, Washington in 1956 from the U.S. Government. It had been a lookout during WWII for enemy ships and subs. Warren enlarged "The Cabin" over the ensuing years to provide more living and sleeping space. What a blessing it has provided for family members for 65 years and counting.

The Cabin (Kalbach's Cove)

The cabin sits in solitude
    Where not so long ago
The sounds of happy voices echoed
    From the beach below.
There, youngsters searched among the rocks
    For treasures of the deep
While parents took their refuge
    In an hour or two of sleep.

Another year of visits
    As the ferryboat arrives
Bringing with it to the cabin
    A kaleidoscope of lives.
The cabin waits for all who come;
    Their spirits to renew.
It makes no difference who you are,
    The cabin welcomes you.

Among the eaves the swallows swoop
    And dive to build their nests.
As morning bursts, they are the first
    To welcome sleeping guests.
A deer may wander through the yard
    In early morning hour,
And quail are seen while visiting
    The green adjacent bower.

A heron claims a rock below;
    An eagle claims the sky,
But seagulls far outnumber here
    The other birds that fly.
The floating kelp, ordained to help
    The otter and the cod,
Appears to be a water tree
    Especially made by God.

Most take their lunches on the deck
    Where there's a folding chair.
The food somehow tastes better
    When it's in the open air.
The days are your ideas;
    Climb the hill or take a walk;
Use the deck to get a suntan
    Or the shade to sit and talk.

While some might row to Deadman's Bay;
   Adventure on their mind,
There'll usually be someone like me
   Whose more inclined to find
A place where agates hide
   Among the multicolored rocks,
And warm sand welcomes feet
   That have grown tired of shoes and socks.

Someone may call, "The whales are here!",
   And all who were at rest
Will quickly scramble to the place
   They find the viewing best.
For sighting of the Orca
   Brings spontaneous applause,
And times when their performance
   Will elicit "Oohs" and "Aahs".

Some nights the guitars will appear
   And singing fills the air.
Or roasting hot dogs on the beach
   With something warm to wear.
Each person has a favorite place
   At night when they retire.
For some it's sleeping in the loft;
   Some by the open fire.

Then all too soon the time arrives
    For guests to say goodbye.
You can't ignore reality
    No matter how you try.
The packing and the cleaning
    Are a part of the routine.
You want the cabin ready
    For the next guests on the scene.

Then once again the rabbits
    Will reclaim their habitat,
While the island waits for summer
    To extend the welcome mat.
The old potbellied stove that warmed
    The guests will sit at ease.
The doors are locked; the place secured
    Against the wintry breeze.

Some dream of being famous
    Or desire what riches bring.
Some do a lot of traveling
    And see a lot of things.
But there's no place I'd rather be
    If I were free to rove
Than the cabin with the ones I love,
    At peace in Kalbach's Cove.

The beginning of great things

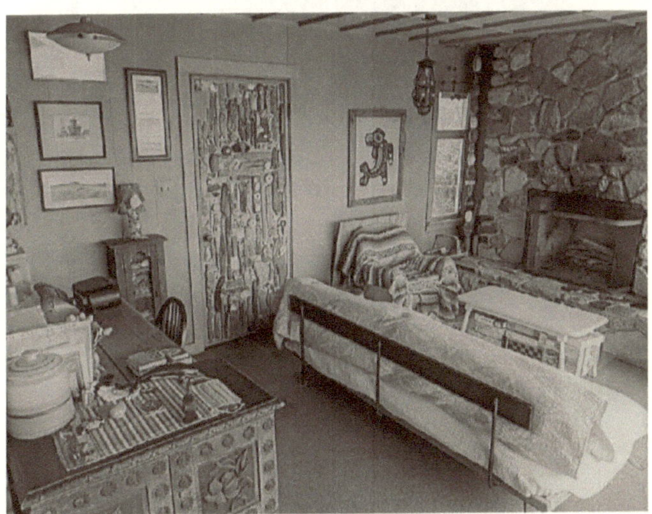

We have arrived!

Tim tending to the Float Forest

While just beyond lay the floating forest

"Hey, anyone seen Mom? We're hungry!"

"Hey, we're hungry, too!"

Food tastes better on the deck

True, but even mussels? "I dare you!"

"Personally, I prefer really fresh salmon."

And top it all off with some music

Alas, all good things must come to an end

But we'll be back, by land <u>and</u> by sea

Part 6
POTPOURRI

Assorted McCreadys, Kalbachs and Hoffmans

Sister Mary's birthday celebration in Canada

Cabin waiting for the next guests to arrive

Oh, good – it's the McCreadys and Cooks!

Clean Routine

The alarm goes off beside my bed.
It rattles round inside my head.
I grope to shut it off for fear
It wakes the dear to whom I'm wed.

My mind slowly shifts into gear
As straining through the dark, I peer
To find my glasses placed nearby
To help my eye to see more clear.

Hot water is in good supply
As soap and shampoo I apply,
Then lose myself in time and space;
A moment's grace to fortify.

I pull the razor cross my face
As if somehow I might erase
The little hairs that surface there
And leave skin bare without a trace.

I brush my teeth and comb my hair;
Choose carefully the clothes to wear.
So my good wife won't think me strange
I always change my underwear.

And so begins another day;
A route from which I seldom stray.
Why burden you with my routine?
So mom will know I'm keeping clean.

Peanut Butter Cookies

Peanut butter is a winner
   Whether breakfast, lunch, or dinner;
A delight to please the palate most agree.
And when brought into obedience
   Mixed with other fine ingredients,
It is worthy of a peanut pedigree.

The cookie that I'm baking
Is by all means worth the taking
Off some time from work like children playing hooky.
Such a winning combination;
   One of infinite creation,
Is the one and only Peanut Butter Cookie.

They're a light and golden brown,
   And well-known all over town
For their tattooed look from fork-implanted ridges.
Looking something like a button,
   Or some clothing after cuttin'
Which was sewn back with those crissy-crossy stitches.

They have tantalizing flavor
   Which brings startling behavior
From grown men and women all across the nation.
Just one whiff of their aroma
   From New York to Arizona
Is enough to start a cookie celebration.

It's no longer any mystery
   Why this cookie's making history,
For the master's touch has all the bakers buzzin'.
It's a product of perfection,
   So, with no further objection
I'll just stop and now devour a baker's dozen.

Perfect for breakfast, lunch, or dinner

Decisions

I love to watch the falling snow
  While I'm inside and dry.
The flakes don't know which way to go,
  But then neither do I.

I thought about my going out
  When thoughts were still unclear.
But with my mind in gear, I find
  I'd rather stay right here.

Decisions, decisions ...

Finding Time

I'd fish today if I had the time.
Shoes kicked off; dropped in line.
I'd sit on the bank in the warm sunshine
If I only had the time.

If I had the time I'd phone a friend;
A helping hand I'd try to lend;
A broken friendship I would mend
If I only had the time.

If I had the time I'd sit a spell
Out on the porch where I could tell
The time of the year just by the smell,
If I only had the time.

If I had the time I'd take a stroll;
A path without another soul
To see what lies just beyond the knoll,
If I only had the time.

Excuses sure are used a lot
To keep from doing things we ought,
Like T's to cross and I's to dot
When we only take the time.

So, I'll take the time to rhyme a poem
About my friends, and fun, and home,
And places I would like to roam
As I stop to take the time.

I worked at Alaska Airlines for ten years with Jerry
McCornack, a retired pastor. We sat at the same 'pod' booking
flights in Reservations. I read this poem to him at his
retirement celebration back in 1996.

Jerry McCornack's Retirement

He came here 'bout ten years ago,
This 'Jerry-atric' so-and-so.
The first two years he couldn't fail.
They put him downstairs sorting mail.

Then thinking he could handle more
They moved him up another floor.
For eight more years he fooled us all.
You'd think he'd really found his call.

A keyboard placed at his command
Was just like putty in his hand.
He sat there grinning with delight
While most his hair was turning white.

At times he'd fall asleep awhile
Until I'd see him start to smile.
Then usually wake up with a jerk
And tell me how he loved his work.

Oh, he sold a flight or two each day
Enough to earn retirement pay.
He says he'll now be building homes
Instead of answering telephones.

I'll miss our games of "Name That Tune"
When things would slow each afternoon.
I really hate to see him go,
This 'Jerry-atric' so-and-so.

Jerry-atric so-and-so McCornack

*This was written back in 1995 before there were actually
churches that rented space in malls to meet on Sundays.*

The Shopping Mall

$$$$

What is it about shopping malls
    That people find so appealing?
Is it all those teens in designer jeans
    That presents a youthful feeling?
Where the elders come for their morning run
    In the hopes of staying fit,
And the mothers shop with the kids while Pop
    Finds another place to sit.

What is it about shopping malls
    That attract so many folks?
Where the children run, and the crying's done,
    And the school kids share their cokes.
Here, the merchants feel they can make a deal
    When their stores are open late.
And the movies play for the ones who stay
    For the last show with their date.

Now the malls provide everything inside,
    Where we used to shop downtown.
There you'd tend to get extremely wet
    When the weather wore a frown.
Now everything is carpeted
    And temperature-controlled.
You can use the 'green' or a bank machine
    Where your card's as good as gold.

You can find the thing to fulfill a dream
    With the wave of a magic wand.
There's a store to meet your every need
    And a few to go beyond.
You'll find picture frames and video games,
    And food of every description.
Shoe repair; they'll style your hair,
    And fill your next prescription.

There are toys galore at the children's store,
    And film processed in an hour.
There's clothes and shoes, and chocolate chews,
    And gifts for a baby's shower.
There's a new display every other day,
    And a sale for each occasion.
There's a form to sign on the dotted line -
    'Win a One Week Free Vacation'.

'Bout the only thing I haven't seen
    Is a place to sit and pray.
But as fast as things are changing now
    That could happen any day.
Someday there'll come a preacher man
    Who will say he has a 'call'
To be ministering the Gospel
    At the First Church of the Mall.

Just be careful my friend in the time you spend
    In the shops and in the hall.
What starts as fun is addicting to some
    At their favorite shopping mall.

This poem is fictitious, but I did borrow the name Josey from a granddaughter. Peasley Canyon and Renton are real places, but not near any border as I imply. I used to drive Peasley Canyon road daily to work in Federal Way, Washington when I taught at the Evergreen State School of Driving.

The Mission (Josey Poe)

Josey Poe was walking slow
   Along the Peasley Canyon
When up ahead he spied a shed
   Which looked to be abandoned.
To be alone as he was prone
   Was not a wise decision,
But here he was, alone, because
   He had a dangerous mission.

The mission known to him alone,
   Since he had no companion
Would come to light this moonlit night
   Down deep in Peasley Canyon.
It seems there was some foul play
   Back in Renton by the river.
The news had spread, some men were dead,
   And folks were all aquiver.

Now people said the killer fled
    To hide from law and order.
The shortest route without a doubt
    Was just across the border.
And Peasley Canyon had to be
    The route that he would travel,
So, Josey Poe was picked to go,
    The mystery to unravel.

To make things worse an evil curse
    As wrought by superstition
Was placed around this wooded ground
    To jeopardize his mission.
Although Sir Josey Poe was not
    A superstitious fellow
A walk through Peasley late at night
    Could turn your legs to jello.

An eerie light shown through the night;
    It cast a gruesome pallor.
Each step he took, although he shook,
    Became a step of valor.
The trees reached out as if to shout
    And stop him from proceeding.
No turning back; ahead the shack;
    There now was no retreating.

Poe stole a glance as if by chance
    He heard something behind him.
He tried to keep himself so low
    That not a soul could find him.
Then suddenly he heard the sound
    Of footsteps in the hollow,
And though he thought that he should stop
    He knew he had to follow.

The footsteps led him straight towards
    The shack inside a clearing.
And now he was confronted
    With the thing he had been fearing.
For there inside Sir Josey spied
    Some thing so terrifying
That just from fright his hair turned white
    As if from instant dyeing.

What Josey saw inside that shack
    May never be discovered.
One thing is known for certain;
    Josey Poe has not recovered.
He stumbles through the streets at night
    In Renton by the river,
And those who see his face say
    It's enough to make one shiver.

So, if you find yourself inclined
   To stroll through Peasley Canyon,
Do so with care, take with you there
   A friend as a companion.
And should you come upon a place
   Where sits a lonely shed,
Remember Poe, and all you know
   From this dumb poem you read.

Where's a friend when you need one?

Letter to Robert Frost

My Dear Mr. Frost,

Though our paths have never crossed
I am prone to hope you are a kindred spirit.
In your poem, "The Road Not Taken"
I can't help but be awakened
Every time that I'm inclined to read or hear it.

Did you think that in your writing
Some would find it so inviting
That it brought to mind life choices they had made?
Education? Occupation?
What's their final destination?
Did they hear the Holy Spirit when they prayed?

On the road we each will travel
There's a time when things unravel
And we'll question if we made the right decision.
That may not have been your purpose
But when brought forth to the surface
It might be a confirmation of our vision.

So, in closing I'm proposing
There are folks with second thoughts,
And they're wondering if the poet was mistaken.
And I'm curious to know
If you ever chose to go
Back once more to explore "The Road Not Taken".

A fellow traveler,
    Jon McCready – 2020

"Choose wisely!"

The Twilight Café (Song)

(Chorus)
Out at the Twilight Cafe on the island;
Snug in the cabin above Kalbach's Cove.
Everyone shares in the songs and the laughter.
Everyone there is so happy to be there.

(Verses)
They fly in from Charleston; they drive from Eugene.
They keep a sharp eye on the clock.
From Renton and Auburn, and Kittitas too,
They all arrive safe at the dock.

The gang from Port Townsend may come the next day.
You never know what they have planned.
But with each arrival there's plenty to do,
So, everyone's lending a hand.
(Chorus)

The ferry boat sails to the island San Juan
Where each person gathers their things.
Then off to the cabin to unlock the doors,
And unload what each family brings.

The kayaks and canoe all land on the beach;
Secure there but ready to float.
There's driftwood to gather, and pools to explore,
And a guestbook for adding a note.
(Chorus)

We'll visit the ranks of the British and Yanks.
Each camp has a story to share.
A pig found some freedom 'til someone done seen 'um;
Now bacon for breakfast was rare.

They brought in the Kaiser to end the dispute.
He pondered, then proffered a plan.
The pig was devoured, and after he'd showered,
He said, "Uncle Sam, you're the man."
(Chorus)

A drive to Roche Harbor to take in the scene;
The Colors, the gardens, the yachts.
A hike up Mt. Young where the view's simply grand.
And the camera? Oh dear, you forgot?

Blackberries for picking; a pie to be baked.
A puzzle to work when it's time.
There's Orcas for sighting; sunsets so inviting
On deck with a bottle of wine.
(Chorus)

Now, some will relax with a book or a sax,
While others may just start to fade.
The poet won't write any verses tonight,
But he may sing a sweet serenade.

So, pull up a chair and forget about life.
It's a good thing to do now and then.
And if you like it here then I have an idea.
Next summer let's all meet again.
(Chorus)

Welcome to Friday Harbor!

Welcome to the Cabin!

Welcome to yumm!

Welcome to the cove!

Welcome to Roche Harbor!

Welcome to "Aaaaaahs..."!

Welcome to conversations!

Welcome to the whales...

... and their tails!

Welcome to close encounters ...

... but *please* don't come any closer!

Index of Titles

Acknowledgements

I am so very grateful to have had the help and support from several family members in compiling, arranging, correcting, and enhancing these poems that I have enjoyed writing over the course of some 70 years.

> ➢ Garry and Carolyn McCready spent many hours loading the poems on computer files and researching printing options to help keep costs to a minimum. Very time consuming, but such a blessing. They made this happen. Can't thank you and Eugene, Oregon enough.
> ➢ With the decision to include pictures to accompany so many poems, Kevin McCready was called upon to explore his many picture albums for appropriate scenes that might enhance the selected items. Thanks so much, Kevin. So glad you have such a good eye.
> ➢ Mark McCready provided the cover photo and helped with pictures and creative ideas as we worked our way through the process. Much appreciated.
> ➢ Linda Lynch took time from her duties as part of the Kent Covenant Church staff to type a number of these poems to better help me get organized in the beginning stages.
> ➢ My wife, Ruth, so often gave me encouragement by her positive comments along the journey.

> And thank you, Lord Jesus, for giving me a love for words that enable me to tell some of my story in ----- MY TIME TO RHYME

The Author

While chopping wood to warm my home,
Or choosing words to write a poem,
To see a smile upon my face
You'll know I'm in my Happy Place.

About the Author

This 87-year-old author is privileged to be the husband of his life-long love, Ruth Eileen Reinke McCready; the father of five wonderful children (Mark, Kevin, Garry, Timothy, and Jennifer); blessed to be grandfather to nine grandchildren, twelve great-grandchildren, and so far, one great-great-grandchild, all of which live in the Pacific Northwest.

In my leisure time, I enjoy working crossword puzzles, jigsaw puzzles, reading novels and biographies, spending time in the San Juan Islands and on the Oregon Coast with family, and exploring new travel destinations.